Don't Touch Me There

Author: **Reese Wordlaw-Outsey**

Co-Author: **Faith Hawkins**

Illustrated By
Rizwan Jani

To: _____

From: _____

Date: _____

I dedicate this book to all the wonderful sons and daughters of this world. May your essence continue to be cherished and protected.

To my amazing daughters Angel, Charity, Faith and my lovely granddaughter, London. May you continue to walk in your purposes with love, faith and boldness.

Hello friends, my name is Cassie. It is short for Cassandra.

I am a little girl and I am four years old.

I might be a little girl, but I know what I want and do not want.

I can give a strong yes and a powerful no.

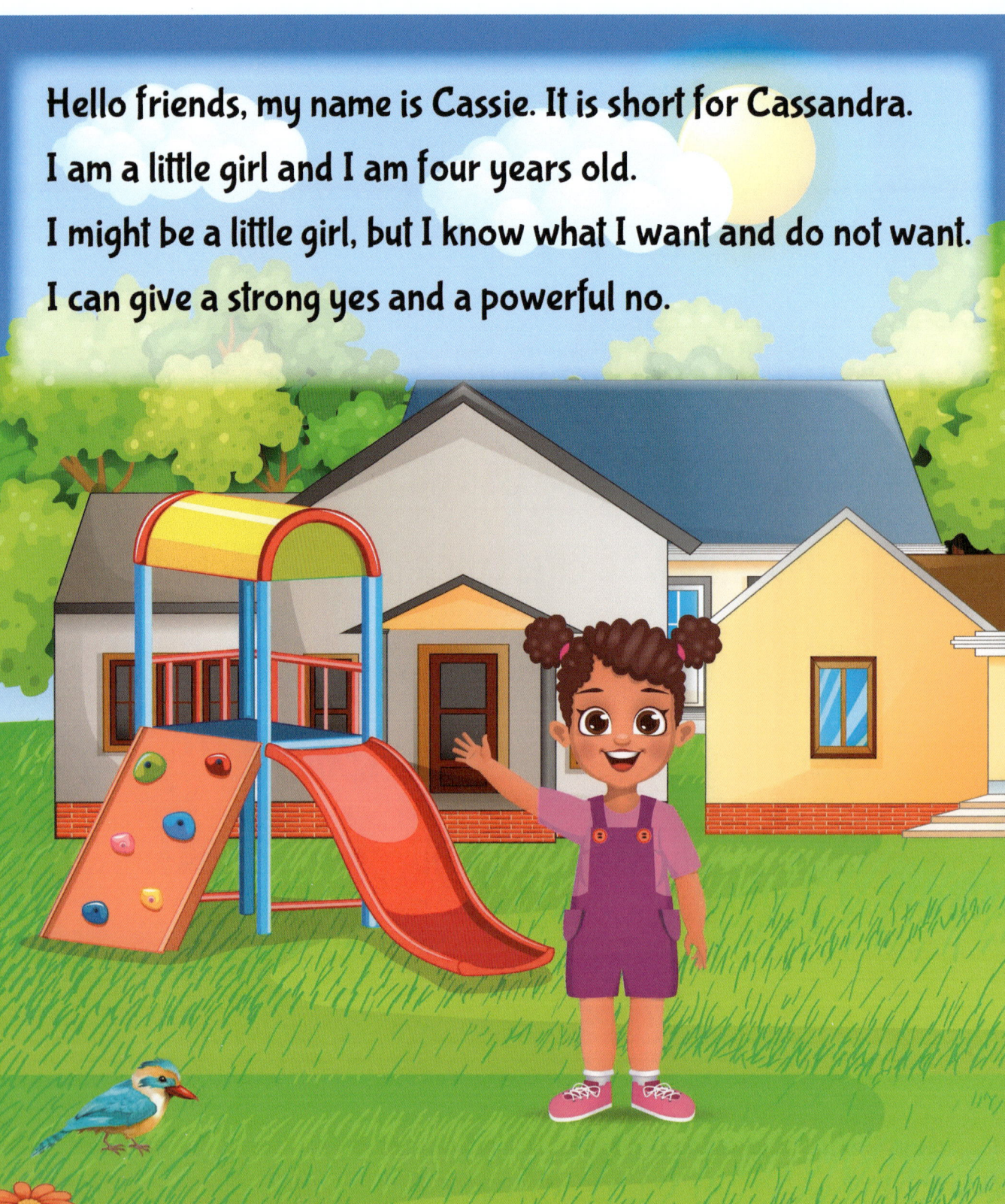

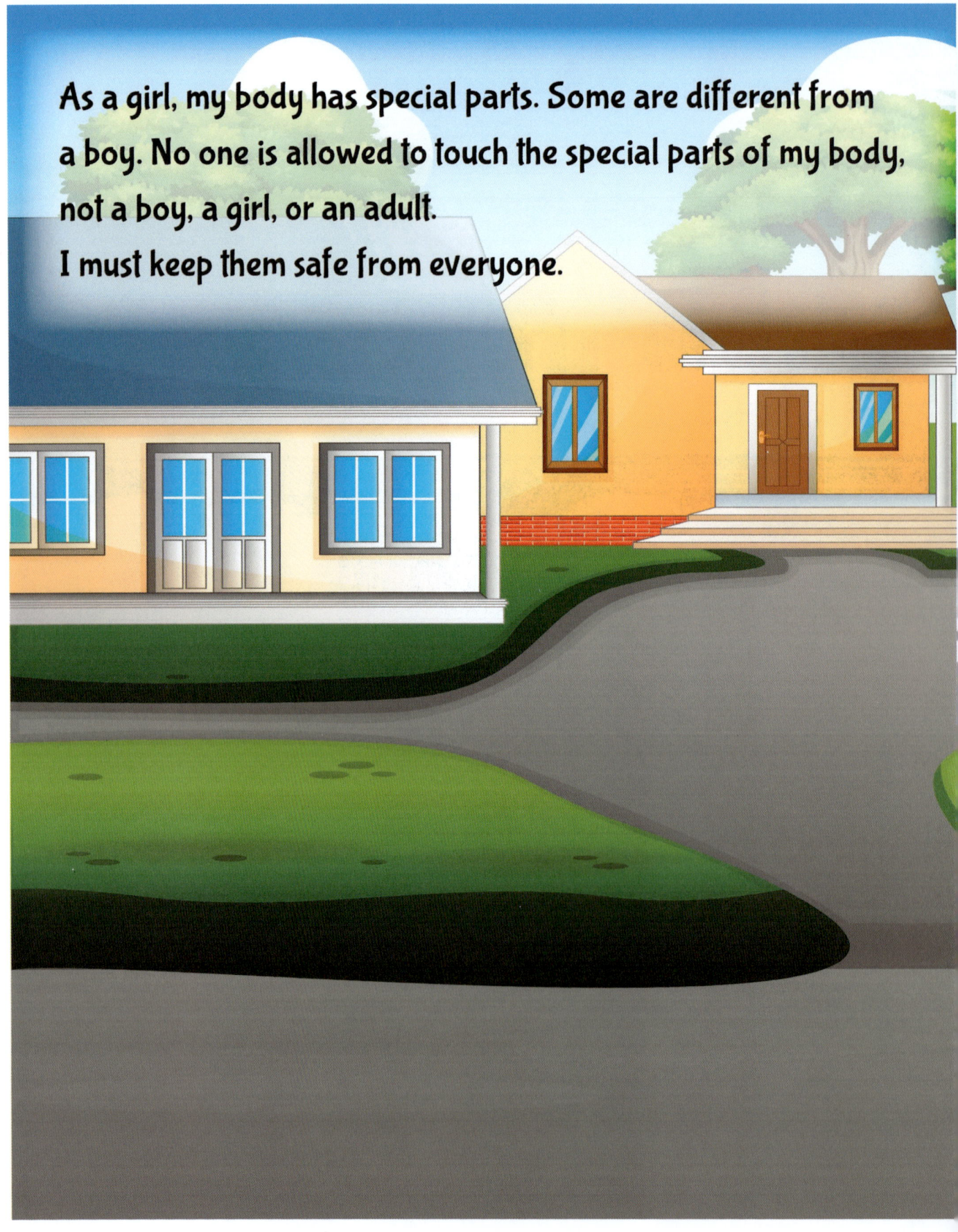

As a girl, my body has special parts. Some are different from a boy. No one is allowed to touch the special parts of my body, not a boy, a girl, or an adult.
I must keep them safe from everyone.

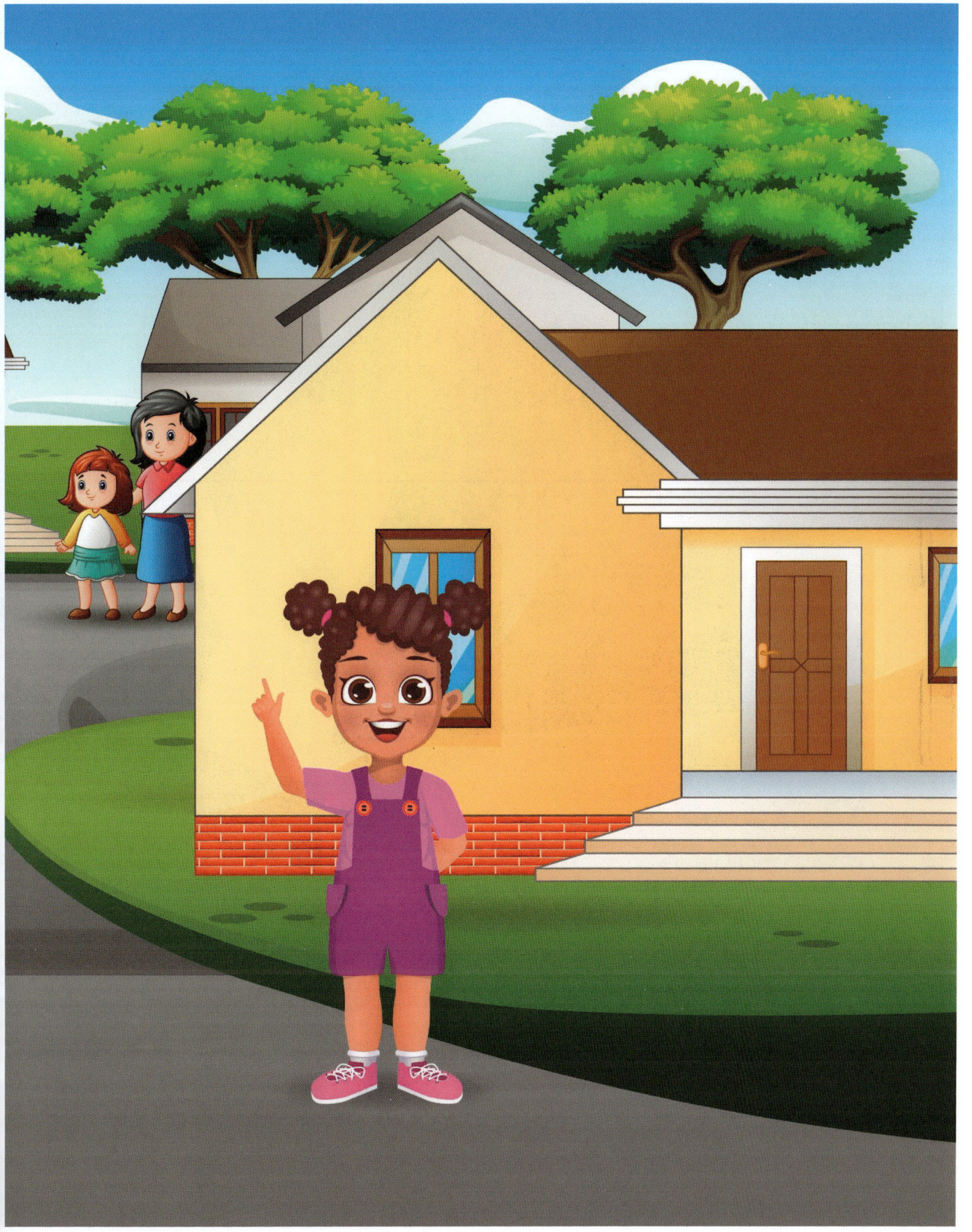

Here is my chest, when I am a bigger girl, it will grow. If someone tries to touch me here, I will tell an adult and say, "NO, don't touch me there, that is my special place and I will go tell."

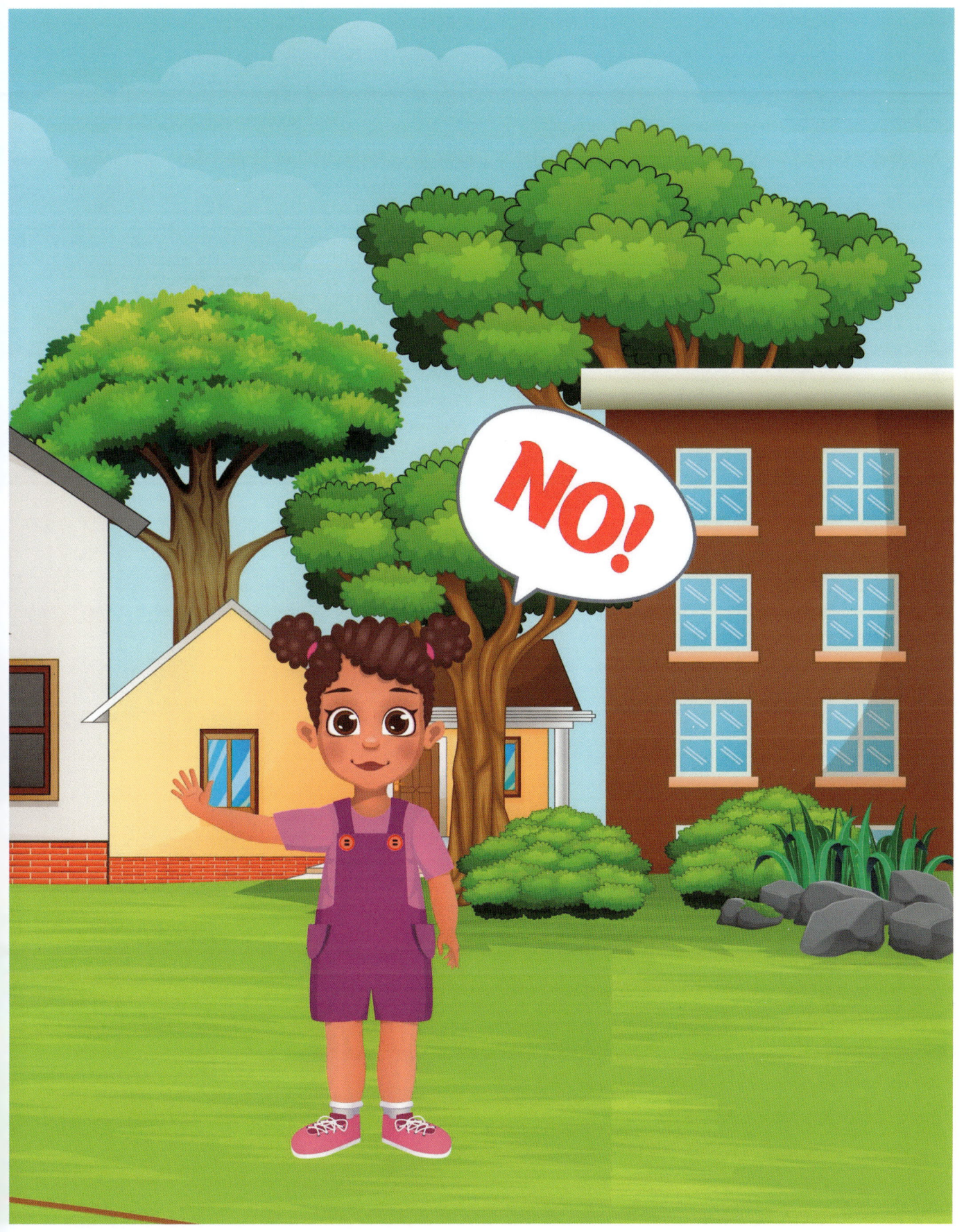

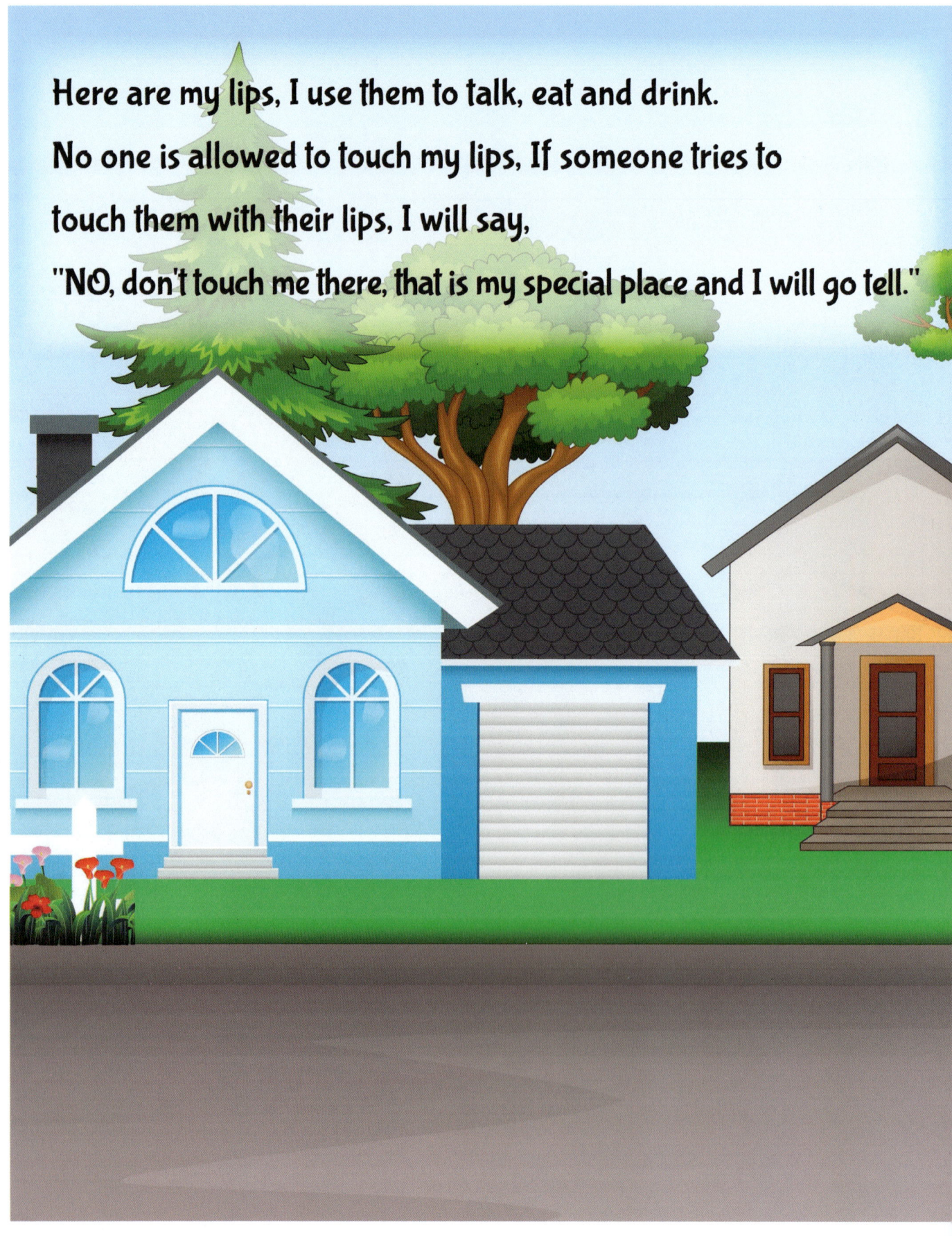

Here are my lips, I use them to talk, eat and drink. No one is allowed to touch my lips, If someone tries to touch them with their lips, I will say, "NO, don't touch me there, that is my special place and I will go tell."

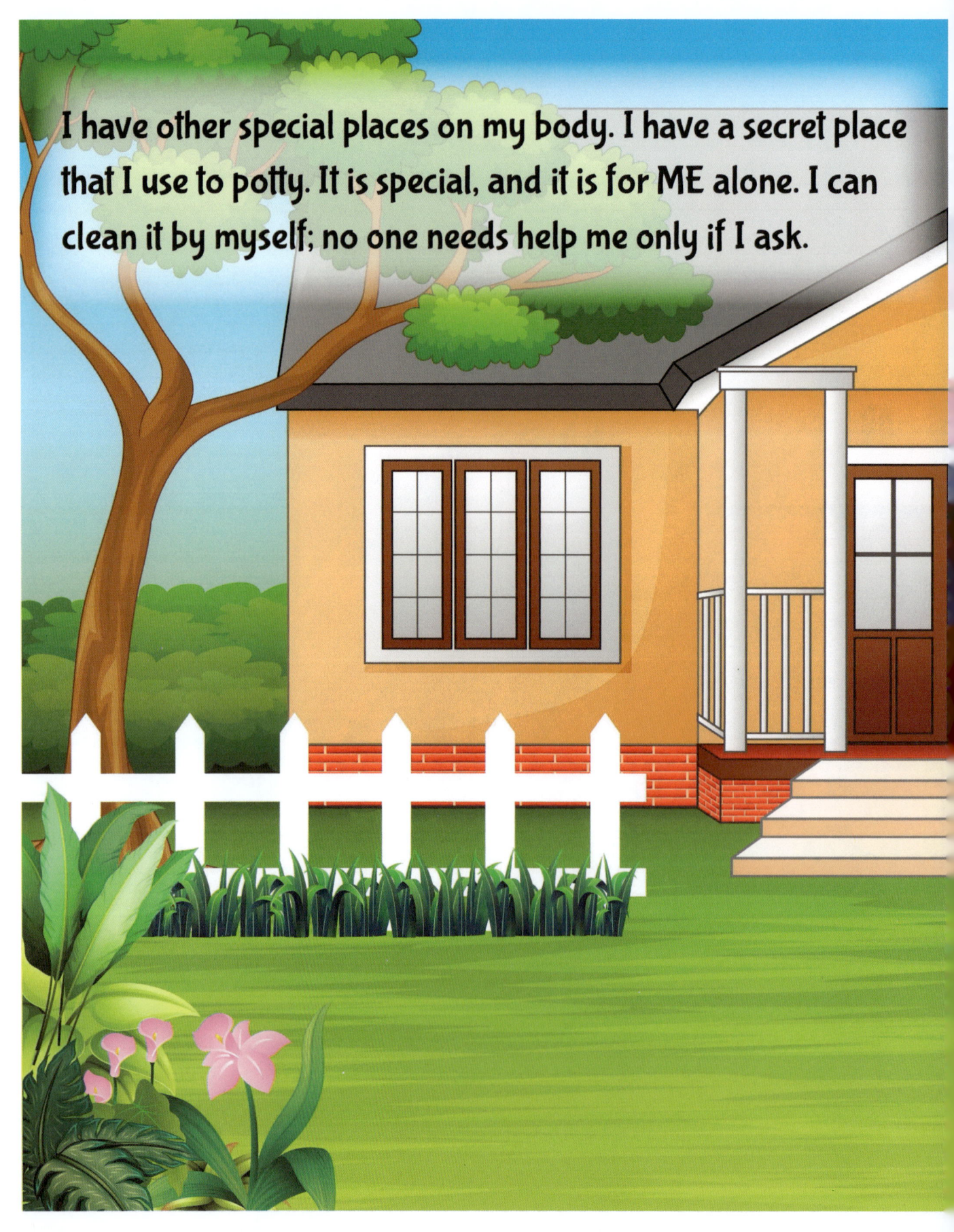

I have other special places on my body. I have a secret place that I use to potty. It is special, and it is for ME alone. I can clean it by myself; no one needs help me only if I ask.

No one is allowed to see or touch my special parts. If someone tries to touch me there, I will say,
"NO, don't touch me there, that is my special place and I will go tell.

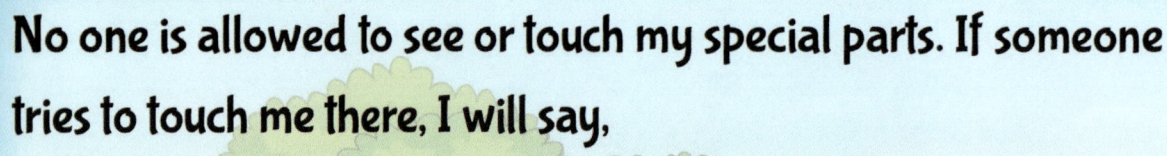

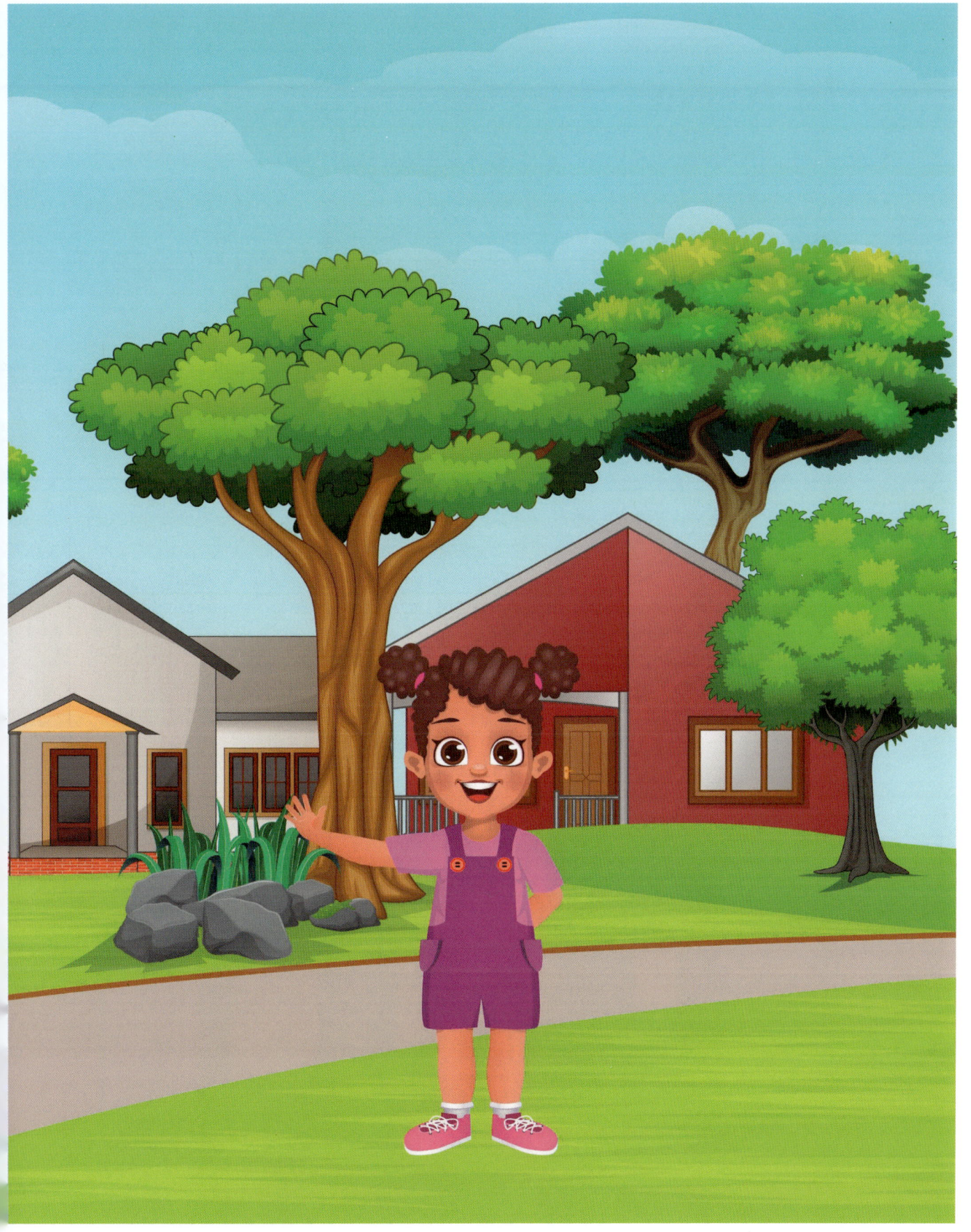

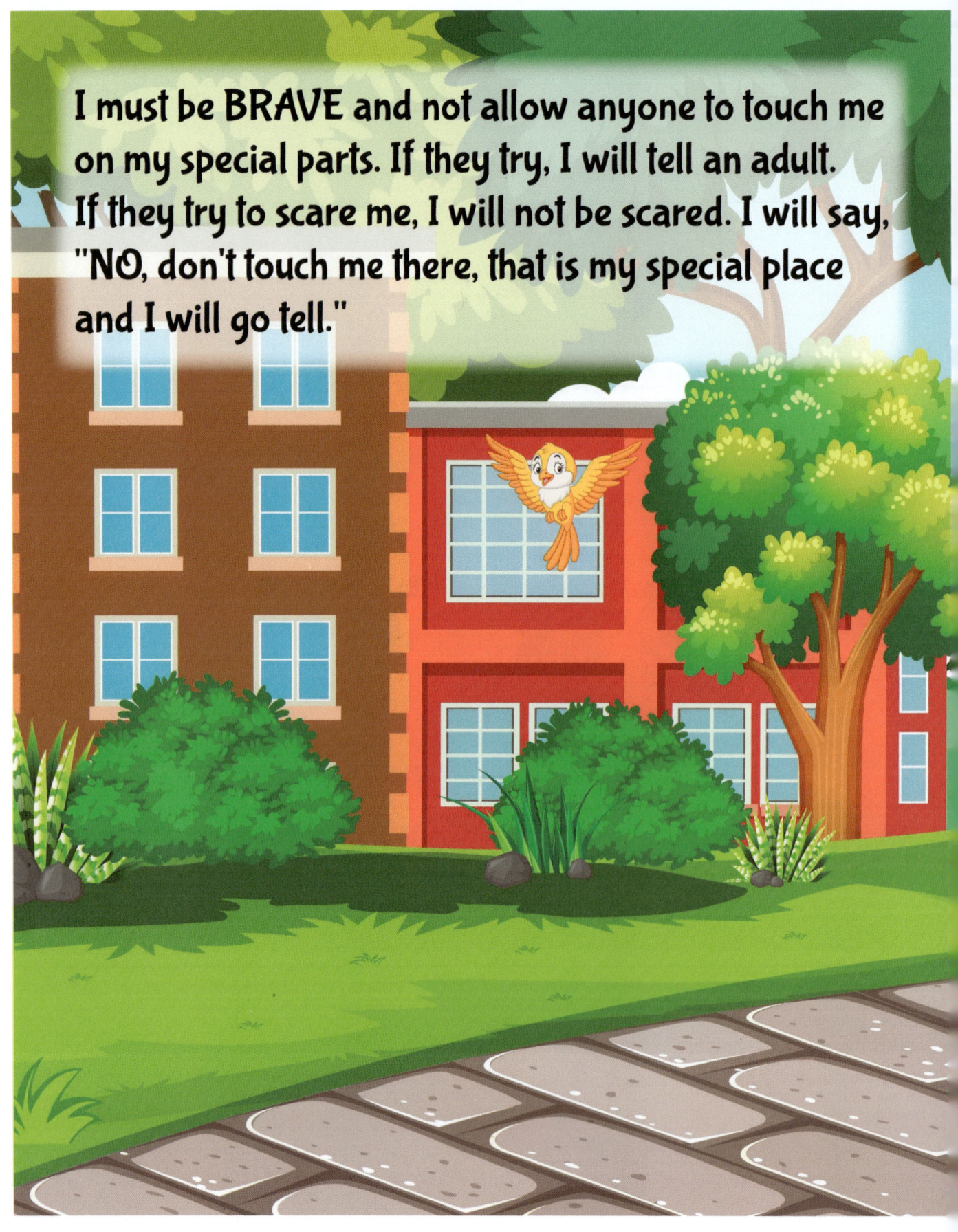

I must be BRAVE and not allow anyone to touch me on my special parts. If they try, I will tell an adult. If they try to scare me, I will not be scared. I will say, "NO, don't touch me there, that is my special place and I will go tell."

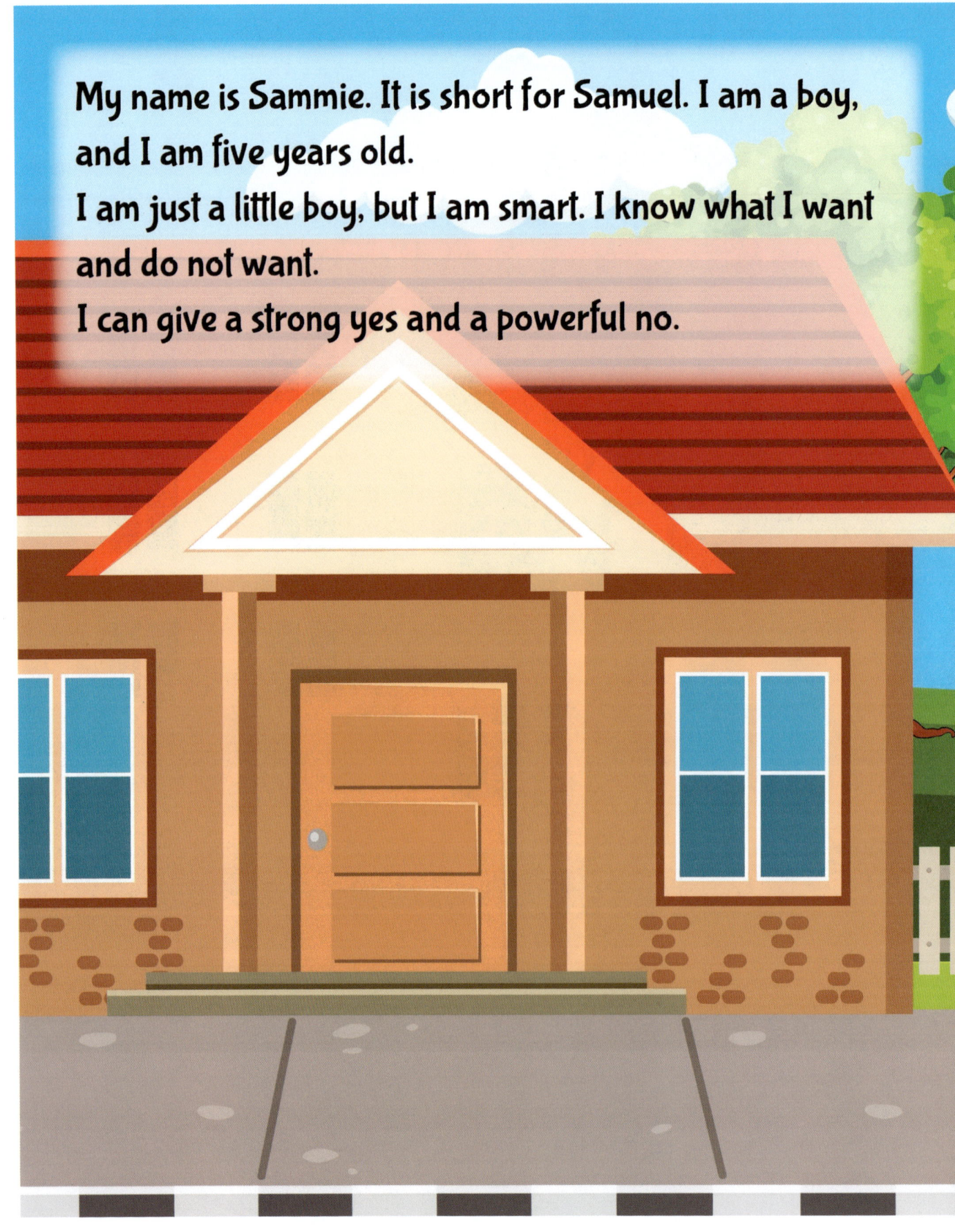

My name is Sammie. It is short for Samuel. I am a boy, and I am five years old.

I am just a little boy, but I am smart. I know what I want and do not want.

I can give a strong yes and a powerful no.

No one is allowed to touch the special parts of my body, not a boy, a girl, or an adult. I must keep them safe from everyone. They are special parts for me alone. I must not let anyone look at them or touch them.

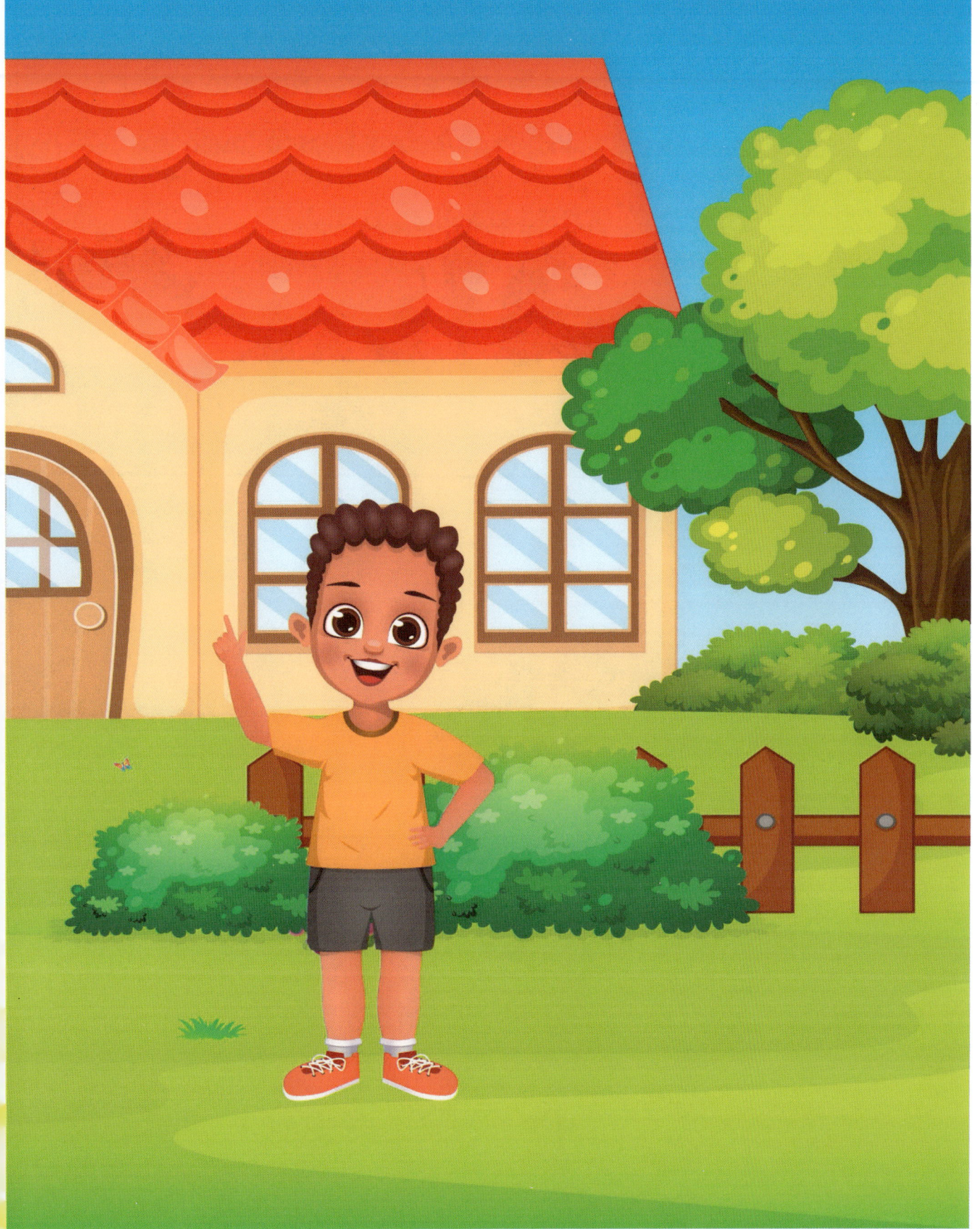

Here are my lips, I use them to talk, eat and drink. No one is allowed to touch my lips, When someone tries to touch them with their lips, I will say,
"NO, don't touch me there, that is my special place and I will go tell."

I have other special places on my body. I use them both to potty. They are special, just for me. I can clean them by myself; no one needs help me unless I ask.

No one is allowed to see or touch the special places on my body, not a boy, a girl, or an adult. If someone tries to look or touch me there, I will say,

"NO, don't touch me there, that is my special place and I will go tell."

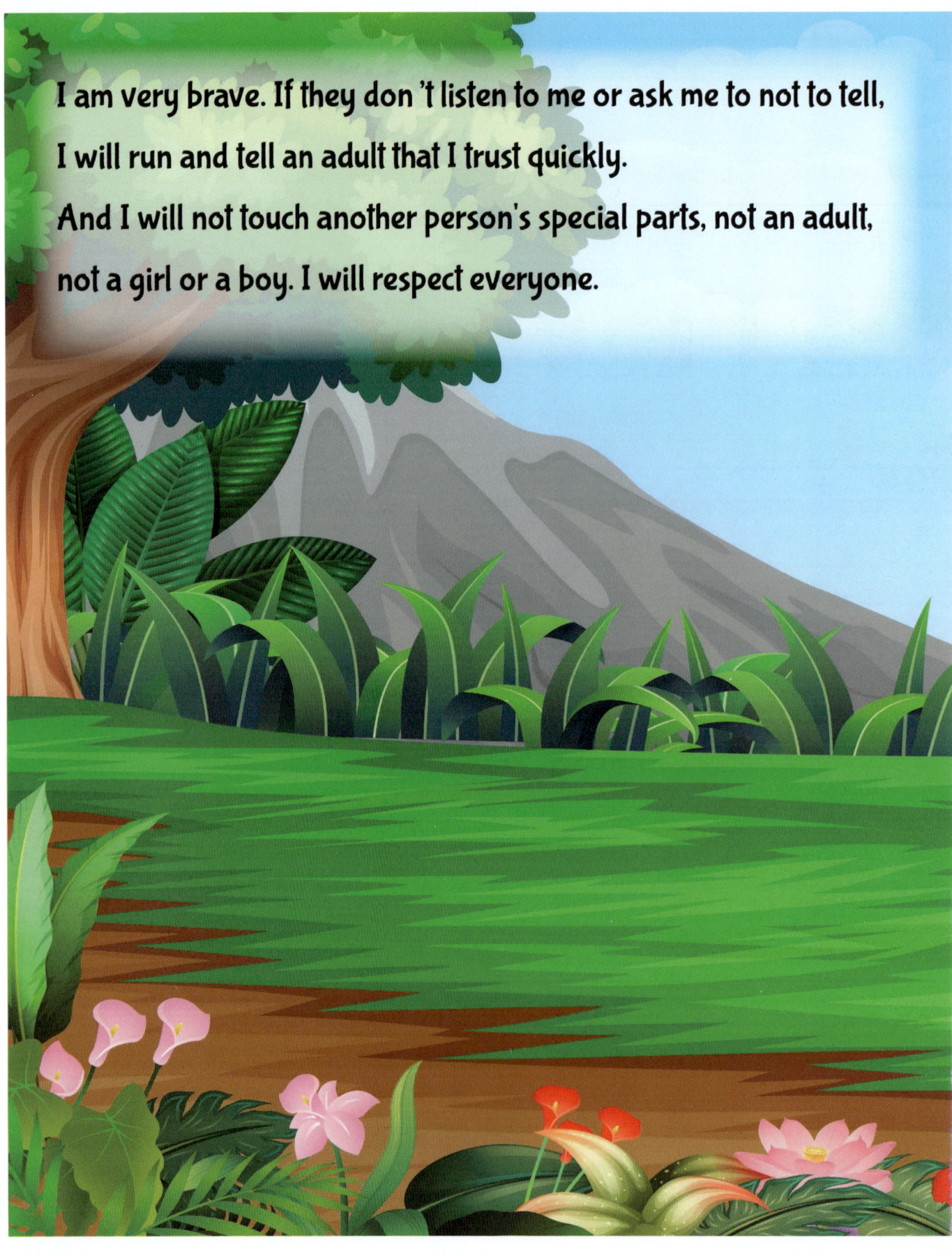

I am very brave. If they don't listen to me or ask me to not to tell, I will run and tell an adult that I trust quickly.

And I will not touch another person's special parts, not an adult, not a girl or a boy. I will respect everyone.

The End

Printed in Great Britain
by Amazon